FORENSIC Investigations

FACT OR FICTION

Looking at forensic investigations and technologies

Leela Burnscott

MACMILLAN
LIBRARY

First published in 2009 by
MACMILLAN EDUCATION AUSTRALIA PTY LTD
15–19 Claremont Street, South Yarra 3141

Visit our website at www.macmillan.com.au or go directly to www.macmillanlibrary.com.au

Associated companies and representatives throughout the world.

National Library of Australia Cataloguing-in-Publication entry

Burnscott, Leela.

   Fact or fiction : looking at forensic investigations and technologies / Leela Burnscott.

   ISBN 978 1 4202 6728 0 (hbk.)
   Includes index.
   Burnscott, Leela. Forensic investigations.
   For primary school age.
   Forensic sciences - Juvenile literature. Evidence (Criminal) - Juvenile literature.

63.25

Edited by Georgina Garner
Text and cover design by Cristina Neri, Canary Graphic Design
Page layout by Raul Diche
Photo research by Sarah Johnson
Illustrations by Alan Laver, Shelly Communications

Printed in China

Acknowledgements
The author and the publisher are grateful to the following for permission to reproduce copyright material:

Front cover photograph: Scene of crime officers (SOCOs) walking along the boundary of a crime scene. The SOCOs are wearing protective clothing in the form of paper suits, overshoes and masks to prevent contamination of the crime scene and any evidence collected. SOCOs provide scientific support to police forces. They establish what evidence is required from a crime scene and the best way to obtain it © Michael Donne/Science Photo Library/Photolibrary

Background images used throughout pages: fingerprint courtesy of iStockphoto/James Steidl; tweezers courtesy of iStockphoto/ Mitar Holod; forensic investigation kit courtesy of iStockphoto/Brandon Alms.

Images courtesy of: AAP Image/AP, 27; Fairfax Photos/Craig Abraham, 30 (middle left); Image copyright © Forensic Document Examination Services Inc., 20; © Foster and Freeman, 23; Getty Images/Bernard Gotfryd, 29; Getty Images/Damian Dovarganes-Pool, 14, 30 (top right); Getty Images/Dan Trevan/AFP, 4 ; Getty Images/Dorling Kindersley, 17 (top); Getty Images/Popperfoto, 28; Getty Images/Robert Voets/CBS Photo Archive, 5; Getty Images/Rod Millington-Pool, 8; iStockphoto, 26 (top), 30 (bottom left); iStockphoto/James Bowyer, 17 (bottom); iStockphoto/Pali Rao, 16 (left); iStockphoto/Steven Robertson, 15; iStockphoto/Susan Trigg, 16 (top right); iStockphoto/Vladimir Daragan, 16 (bottom right); Images copyright © Human Biosciences, La Trobe University, 21; Andrew Lambert Photography/Science Photo Library/Photolibrary, 18; Mauro Fermariello/Science Photo Library/Photolibrary, 13; Michael Donne/Science Photo Library/Photolibrary, 7, 30 (middle right); Pasquale Sorrentino/Science Photo Library/Photolibrary, 24, 25, 30 (top left); Philippe Psaila/Science Photo Library/Photolibrary, 10; Sheila Terry/Science Photo Library/Photolibrary, 19; Shutterstock/Aguirre_mar, 26 (bottom); Shutterstock/Iofoto, 22; Shutterstock/Loren Rodgers, 6; Shutterstock/Stephen Sweet, 11; Image copyright © Victorian Institute of Forensic Medicine, 12, 30 (bottom right).

While every care has been taken to trace and acknowledge copyright, the publisher tenders their apologies for any accidental infringement where copyright has proved untraceable. Where the attempt has been unsuccessful, the publisher welcomes information that would redress the situation.

Contents

GLOSSARY WORDS

When a word is printed in **bold**, you can look up its meaning in the Glossary on page 31.

Science in the court!

Forensic science is the use of scientific knowledge and techniques within the legal system, particularly in the investigation of crime. Forensic science can:

- determine if an **incident** resulted from an accident, natural causes or a criminal act
- identify those involved in the incident
- identify and find those people responsible for the incident
- make sure that the innocent are not wrongly convicted.

The term 'forensic science' is quite misleading because it suggests only one type of science is involved. This is certainly not the case. Forensic investigations can involve virtually every field of science and technology, from electronics to psychology.

Forensic investigations require the skills of specially trained police, scientists, doctors, engineers and other professionals. These investigators examine all types of evidence, from bloodstains to weapons and from bugs to computers. The greater the pool of evidence against an accused person, the greater the chance of a conviction.

A forensic expert presents crime scene photographs during a trial.

Fact or fiction?

Turn on the television any night of the week and there is bound to be at least one forensic show on. In these shows, even the worst crimes take only a few days to solve, thanks to clever, hard-working forensic scientists and police. Unfortunately, in reality, it is not that simple. It can take months or even years to solve a case. In fact, some cases are never solved.

Unlike in television shows, forensic evidence can be misinterpreted or misused. This can cause innocent people to be jailed and guilty people to walk free. To minimise the risk of wrongful convictions and maximise the chance of solving crimes, a forensic investigation must follow strict procedures. These procedures apply at the crime scene, right through to the analysis of evidence in the laboratory.

Sometimes it is hard to tell the difference between fact and fiction on forensic television shows.

Crime scene preservation

The first step in any investigation is to physically and visually **preserve** the crime scene. This is vital. If not done properly, this could result in a case being thrown out of court.

Securing the scene

It is the role of the first police officers on the scene to:

- stop unauthorised people from entering the area
- close off or tape off the area to **secure** it
- keep a record of who comes and goes
- protect any evidence that is likely to be destroyed, disturbed or lost.

This physically preserves the scene and protects evidence from disturbance, **contamination** and being removed or destroyed. The police officers must also immediately call in the detectives who will take over the investigation.

DID YOU KNOW?

Detectives are specially trained police who investigate crimes. They do not wear police uniforms or carry out day-to-day policing duties such as traffic control.

Police often secure a crime scene by taping off the area.

POLICE LINE DO NOT CROSS

Photographing the scene

Photographs visually preserve a scene and provide a permanent record. Videos, sketches and notes can also be used to record the scene, but generally only photos of evidence are presented in court.

Detectives or specially trained police officers take crime-scene photographs. They start with wide-angle shots of the entire scene and the surrounding area, and then slowly move in, taking close-up shots of individual objects and pieces of evidence.

Once the scene has been fully photographed, scene-of-crime officers (SOCOs) can enter and start work. Each time a new **item of interest** is found, it is photographed up close, by itself and then with a ruler or another object next to it. This is used as a scale to show how big the item of interest actually is.

A police photographer wears protective clothing and slippers so he does not contaminate the crime scene.

Collecting evidence

Once the crime scene has been preserved, forensic investigators can start collecting evidence. Evidence is anything that can help explain what happened or that can link people to the crime scene or crime. Forensic evidence includes shoe prints, fingerprints, tool marks, glass fragments, bullets, documents, interviews, e-mails and even insects.

Under the microscope

Strict rules must be followed when collecting evidence so that the evidence will be accepted in court. Many objects used as evidence can be easily picked up and taken back to the laboratory for analysis. Marks, bloodstains and prints need to be analysed at the scene or from photographs. Plaster casts of impressions can be made for analysis back at a laboratory.

Analysis of evidence can involve many different specialists, techniques and instruments. Some techniques and types of evidence are routinely accepted in court, but others are not.

An expert witness examines a piece of evidence in court.

Searching for evidence

To make sure no evidence is missed, police must carry out thorough searches in a coordinated and systematic way. The four main types of search method are:

- spiral search
- grid search
- line search
- zone search.

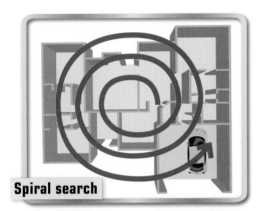
Spiral search

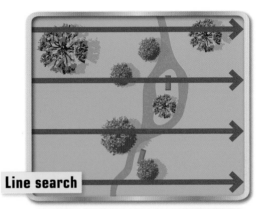
Line search

Grid search

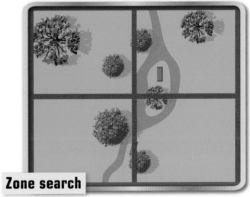
Zone search

The method that is used depends on the site and size of the crime scene.

Spiral searches are mostly used for crimes that occur in a small area, such as in a house. A spiral search either starts from inside the room in which the crime occurred and then spreads outwards, or works from the outside in.

Line searches are used for searching medium-sized areas. This technique is often used for finding evidence in open areas such as parks.

Grid and zone searches are useful for searching very large areas. During a major explosion or plane crash, evidence can be scattered over a very large area.

A scene-of-crime officer places an item in an evidence bag at a crime scene.

Protecting evidence

All evidence collected from a crime scene should be protected so that it is not contaminated, broken, damaged or lost. Each item must be immediately placed in its own evidence bag or container. This is labelled with what evidence is in it, where and when it was found, and who placed it in the container.

Items should not be picked up by hand unless gloves are worn. Forceps, tweezers and other tools are also used to pick up evidence.

If two pieces of evidence are stuck together, they should not be separated. If an item of clothing has plant material stuck to it, this plant material should not be removed. Instead, the clothing and plant material should be packaged together, once a photograph of the evidence has been taken.

Chain of custody

For evidence to be **admissible** in court, it must have an unbroken chain of custody. This is a complete record of everyone who handled the evidence, where the evidence was collected from, where it was transported to and who examined it.

This chain-of-custody system was set up to protect evidence from being lost, changed in any way or touched by people who should not have access to it. Any break in this chain of custody means that a judge will stop the evidence being used in court. This could, of course, destroy an entire case and result in a guilty person walking free.

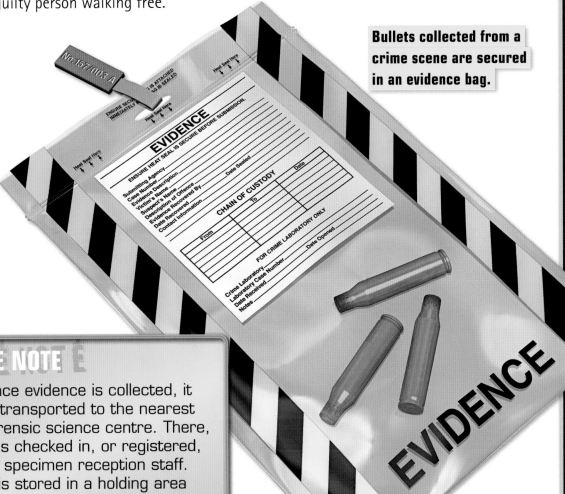

Bullets collected from a crime scene are secured in an evidence bag.

CASE NOTE

Once evidence is collected, it is transported to the nearest forensic science centre. There, it is checked in, or registered, by specimen reception staff. It is stored in a holding area until the appropriate forensic scientist collects it.

Analysing evidence

Unlike the investigators in television shows, most forensic investigators specialise in only one area or field. Evidence may therefore be analysed by more than one forensic specialist.

Forensic experts

By specialising in one area, forensics scientists become experts in that area. Investigators with similar expertise work in the same unit within a forensic science centre.

Forensic science centres are made up of many specialist units, such as:

- the **ballistics** unit, which analyses gun and bullet evidence
- the fingerprint unit, which analyses fingerprints and other body prints
- the document examination unit, which analyses handwriting, inks and paper types
- the **trace evidence** unit, which analyses any material found in very small amounts at a crime scene, such as hairs and soil
- the audio-visual unit, which analyses audio-visual evidence as well as new technologies and digital material.

Different types of forensic scientists may work in the same forensic laboratory.

Sharing the evidence

Analysing evidence is not a quick or simple process. It can take days or even weeks to complete tests and analyse results. Most items of evidence need to be analysed by several different experts, so the evidence is sometimes shared across different units.

A crash investigator examines a car at a forensic science centre.

CASE NOTE

In the case of a single-car crash, the crash investigation team is the first group of experts involved. They examine the scene to work out how the crash happened. Before the car is removed, they look for clues, such as skid marks, and note the force and angle of impact of the car.

The car is then sent to a forensic science centre where the crash investigation team of specialist engineers and mechanics examine it. They look for mechanical faults such as brake problems or balding tyres. Other investigators may also examine the car looking for traces of soil or gravel embedded in the tyres or mismatched paint flakes on the car body. This can help determine if another car was involved in the crash and where the crashed car had been previously.

Presenting evidence in court

For evidence to be admissible in court, it must:

- have an unbroken chain of custody
- be related to the case and prove a certain point
- have been analysed using accepted forensic techniques
- be recorded in photographs and notes to show where or what the evidence came from.

Forensic investigators who present evidence in court are called expert witnesses.

Expert witnesses

Any forensic investigator can be called to court as an expert witness. The role of an expert witness is to explain their scientific findings in a clear, simple and **unbiased** way. They do not decide the guilt or innocence of the person on trial.

Many forensic experts are employed by the government through the police force. Some experts work privately and can be hired by anyone. Researchers from universities or scientific institutes who are experts in a field can also be called to give evidence.

A forensic expert explains evidence in a way that the jury and judge can understand.

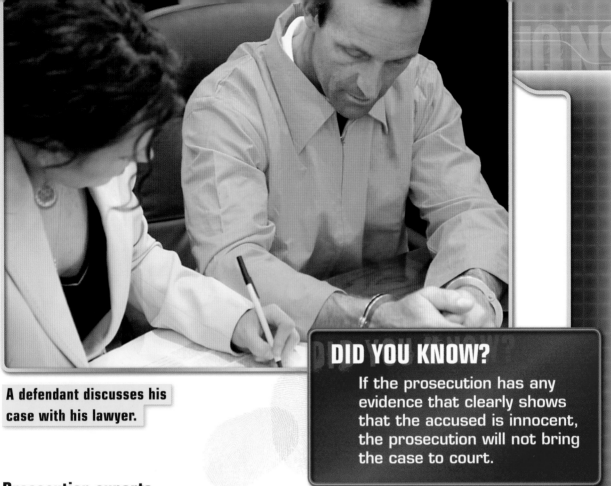

A defendant discusses his case with his lawyer.

Prosecution experts

The prosecution team is the team that brings a criminal case to court. The prosecution usually uses government investigators as expert witnesses. They present evidence that shows that the accused is likely to have committed the offence. Any evidence that does not help prove the case is not presented.

Defence experts

The defence team is the team that represents the accused. The defence often has independent investigators review all the evidence. If they find that the evidence raises doubt over the prosecution's case, these independent investigators will be called as expert witnesses for the defence.

Conflicting opinions

Differences of opinion can occur in forensic investigations, just like in any field of study. This is because different experts use slightly different techniques or interpret results differently. Normally, only proven or widely accepted techniques are allowed in court.

Document analysis

Document analysis is a broad science that covers many different areas of analysis, including the chemical, physical and structural properties of papers and inks. A document can be a scrap of paper, an envelope, a will, paper money, cheques, passports or any other printed material. Document analysis is often used in television crime shows where, for a change, they actually show more fact than fiction.

Revealing the facts

By analysing a document, investigators can determine:

- the document's age
- if the document is an original, copy or fake
- who prepared the document
- where the document came from or where it has been.

This information can help prove if a crime has been committed and, if so, by whom. Document analysis is used in many types of cases, such as forgeries, blackmail cases and kidnap cases, and for dating documents.

If it looks suspicious, a passport may be analysed by a document examiner who will look for fraud.

LAST WILL AND TESTAMENT

I, John Doe, residing at 58 Any Street, Any City, Anywhere do hereby make, publish and declare this to be my Last Will and Testament and hereby revoke ... all Wills and Codicils at any time heretofore made by me.

I direct that the expenses of my funeral and burial [or cremation] ... out of my estate in such amount as my Personal Representative may deem pro... without regard to any limitation in the applicable law or rule of court as to th... of such expenses and without the necessity of court approval.

Money is often examined to check that it is not fake, or counterfeit.

A will may be examined to check that it has not been altered.

Paper analysis

To the naked eye, one piece of paper does not look much different from another. Two pieces of paper, however, can be very different indeed.

What makes papers different are the fibres, glues, dyes and chemicals used to create the paper, as well as the presence of any watermarks. Forensic chemists analyse the individual characteristics of different papers to identify the paper source and batch.

Over the years, the various materials that make up paper have changed. This can help investigators discover the approximate age of a document. The paper of a document that is claimed to have come from the 1700s should not have traces of modern materials in it. If it does, the document is obviously a forgery.

Paper comes in different textures, thicknesses and colours due to the different fibres, glues and chemicals that are used.

A stamp has been placed on top of the watermark in this passport.

DID YOU KNOW?

Watermarks are designs impressed in paper that are only visible when held up to a light source. They are often used in paper money and other important documents as a security measure against forgery.

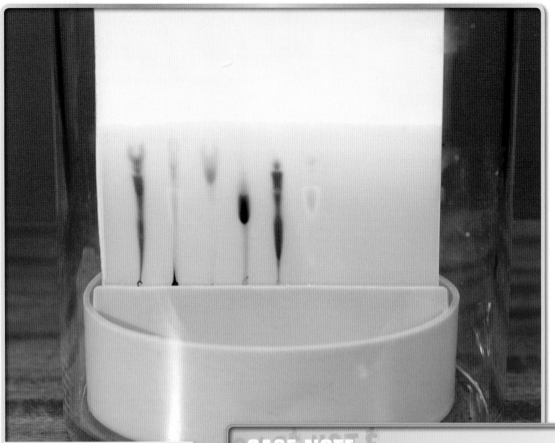

Six different inks are treated with solvent to show how each ink is made up of a different combination of chemical dyes.

Ink analysis

It is hard to tell the difference between two inks of the same colour by sight. Just like paper, however, there are differences in inks that can be used for identification and ageing. These differences include the chemicals and dyes used to make up the inks. Most commercial inks are made up of a unique combination of chemical dyes, which can be separated and analysed easily. Also, many producers now add chemical 'date tags' to their inks so that the exact year of manufacture can be determined. All inks have these different characteristics, including those used in pens, printers, typewriters and photocopiers.

Altered documents

The text on documents is sometimes altered illegally. Alterations could be changing the name of a **beneficiary** on a will or forging a signature on a contract.

One of the most common alterations to a document is to erase part of the original text. This can be done with an eraser, sandpaper, a knife or a razor blade. These types of alterations cause damage to the surface of the paper. Sometimes, the damage is visible to the naked eye, but other times it can only be picked up when seen through a microscope.

Chemicals can also be used to 'white out' the ink. This can often only be detected by placing the document under certain types of light, such as ultraviolet or infrared light.

As well as deleting text, documents can be altered by adding text. By examining documents under infrared and other kinds of light, experts can detect if two different inks were used on the one document. The light shows where any text has been added.

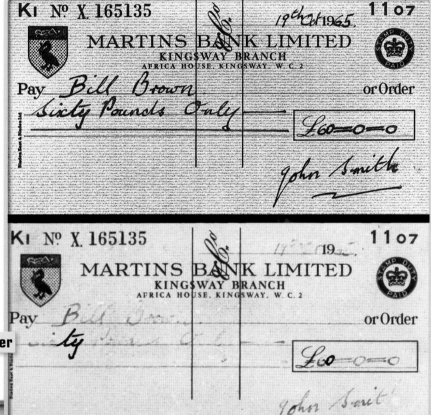

s picture shows an ered cheque seen in mal light.

s picture shows the e cheque with the ered text exposed under aviolet (UV) light.

Handwriting analysis

Experts believe that no two individuals write exactly the same. People may write in very similar styles but each has an individual way of forming and joining letters. Some differences in style are so obvious that even an untrained person can easily pick them. Other differences are much more complex and very difficult to detect.

When handwriting is disguised, the writing is kept as simple and indistinct as possible. This makes style characteristics even harder to detect. Disguised writing is often used in ransom letters or threatening notes.

Handwriting analysis is not a perfect science. Conclusions are very much up to an expert's abilities and opinion. Sometimes it is impossible for an expert to come to any conclusion at all.

A document examiner has marked up a suspect signature that has been carefully traced and then retouched.

Original signature

Forged signature

A document examiner marks the features
of a forged and an original signature.

Detecting handwriting forgeries

Handwriting experts have two main tasks. One is to detect if a document has
been altered, and the other is to determine who wrote or altered a document.

To work out if a document was altered or if it was written entirely by one person,
the examiner must compare the writing throughout the document with itself.
If any differences in style are found, this would suggest that someone else had
altered the original document by adding to it.

To work out who wrote all or parts of a document, the investigators must have
writing samples to compare. Samples from the person who was supposed to have
written the document and from the suspected forger are required. Portions of
each sample are enlarged and placed side by side. The examiner then carefully
looks for individual characteristics of each piece of writing, such as the way
a person always crosses a 't' or writes the tail on a 'g', and compares these
characteristics.

The particular typeface used by a typewriter can be seen in reverse on its typebars.

Print analysis

Analysing differences in typed or mechanically printed documents is also part of a document examiner's job. Before computers and electronic printers, most documents were produced on typewriters. Each kind of typewriter used a particular typeface or font. To identify the specific typewriter used, the forensic examiner looked for individual characteristics and minute imperfections that were unique to a machine. This could be the spacing between letters, the alignment of the letters, the difference in print darkness between letters, or faults in particular letters.

These days, most things are printed on ink-jet printers or laser printers, or copied on fax machines or photocopiers. Individual machine characteristics of electric printers are harder to detect than manual typewriter characteristics. As technologies improve, however, so too do forensic document examination techniques. Traceable characteristics on material printed electronically include differences between printer toners and how the paper is affected as it passes through printer rollers. Tiny print differences made by unique marks on a photocopier's lid or glass can help track down which copier was used to produce a document.

Text impressions

Document examiners do not even need visible print to link a person or machine to a crime. Instead, they can use any imprints left on paper.

When a person writes on a notepad or pile of paper, an imprint of the text they have written is often left on the pages under the page they have written on. Investigators have developed a number of ways to view these imprints. One technique involves placing the document under special lighting conditions and another involves coating the paper with a coloured powder or dye.

Electronic documents

Today, most documents are not printed out but read directly off a computer screen. Music and videos are also played directly from computers instead of from videos, DVDs and CDs. This has led to a new type of crime called e-crime or electronic crime, which includes forgeries and unlicensed copying or pirating of material.

There are now forensic experts highly skilled in all aspects of computers and information technology. These investigators can track down where an e-mail was sent from, where a website is being hosted and which computer was used to pirate material or create a document.

A forensic investigator uses an electrostatic detection apparatus (ESDA) to show up text impressions on paper.

Audio analysis

In forensic science, audio or sound analysis can provide vital clues. Analysis of recordings can pick up faint background noises or conversations that can sometimes help locate the speaker. Voice analysis can also sometimes help identify a speaker.

Background noise

Using specially designed equipment and computer programs, audio specialists can skillfully filter out interfering sounds to make voices or other important sounds much clearer. They can also visualise sound waves and compare them to check if a recording had been altered or edited.

DID YOU KNOW?

Real-life audio specialists are good, but not as good as those that are seen on television. This type of forensic science is often exaggerated in television shows. Real-life audio specialists cannot clean up and amplify a faint background noise to reveal that it is the sound of a particular train leaving a specific station.

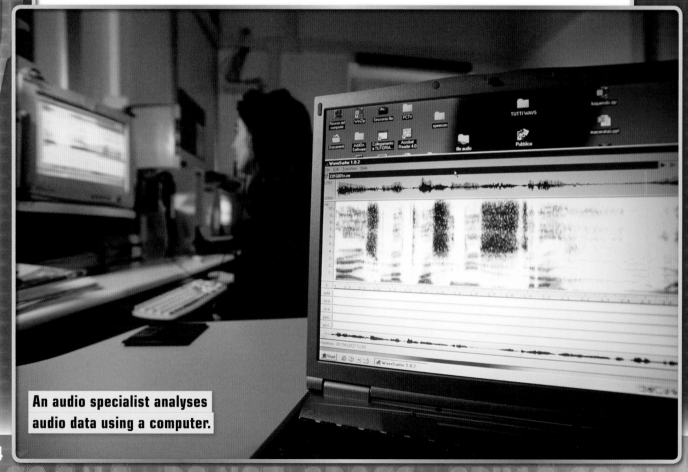

An audio specialist analyses audio data using a computer.

Voice analysis

In 1941, the Bell Telegraph Laboratories in New Jersey, USA, developed the sound spectrograph. A spectrograph is a specialised machine that visualises speech and other sounds. It measures **pitch**, **tone** and volume and represents them as a series of lines. The lines of this 'voiceprint' are analysed and compared to other recordings to try to identify a speaker.

Over the years, this technique has become much more sensitive. Voice analysis, however, is not widely accepted and is only sometimes allowed as evidence in a court of law.

Sound can be visualised using a spectrograph.

DID YOU KNOW?

A study by the US Federal Bureau of Investigation (FBI) in 2000 showed that 31 per cent of all voiceprints examined were wrongly identified and that 53 per cent wrongly excluded the speaker.

Image analysis

Images are widely used in forensic investigations. Video security footage, photographs of crime scenes and images of footprints or fingerprints may be analysed. Most forensic units have a dedicated team of experts whose roles include enhancing image quality and improving matching techniques.

Fingerprints taken from a scene may be of varying quality.

Image comparison

Forensic investigators are always looking to improve the way they compare images of identifying evidence, such as fingerprints, shoe prints and faces, with samples held on **databases**. By developing more sensitive and more accurate computer programs, investigators can cut down their workload and reduce the chance of error.

CASE NOTE

Police forces all over the world have developed their own facial recognition software packages. These are used to digitally create life-like images of a suspect, based on descriptions provided by a victim or witness. In the past, police artists drew these images.

A fingerprint may be enhanced so that it has high contrast and its details can be seen.

2008-03-06   03:40:45a

Image enhancement

In television shows, there is often a whiz technician who can turn a small, blurred blob on video security footage into a clear picture of the culprit. Unfortunately, this is more fiction than fact. When a digital image is enlarged too much, it turns into a pixellated mess.

DID YOU KNOW?

Pixel is short for picture element. The more pixels an image has, the clearer the picture is and the more it can be enlarged. If an image is enlarged too much, all that can be seen is a mess of multicoloured, square pixels.

In reality, only a small proportion of all security footage is useable. Most is of such poor quality that very little can be done to improve it. Poor quality may be caused by the video tape wearing out from repeated use, dirty recording heads or a low-quality recorder.

Improving the quality of images, where possible, makes visual comparison much easier. Experts use specially designed computer programs that improve an image by:

- enhancing the contrast, which is the difference in colour intensities
- altering the brightness or dullness of the image
- increasing the **resolution**
- sharpening or de-blurring the image.

The Howard Hughes hoax

Howard Hughes is pictured here in 1950, before he became a recluse.

Background

Howard Hughes was a famous US billionaire and eccentric. He was a very private man and, after years in the spotlight, he became a **recluse**. This only made him more interesting to the press and public, and he became the subject of many rumours and much gossip.

Clifford Irving was a successful author who had written many best-selling books.

The crime

In 1971, Clifford Irving approached his publisher, McGraw-Hill, with letters he claimed were written by Howard Hughes asking Irving to write his autobiography. Irving's publishers jumped at the idea and wrote up a contract in which Irving would receive US$100 000 and Hughes would receive US$650 000. Irving claimed the reclusive Hughes would not come in person to sign the contract, so it was given to Irving to pass onto him. Irving returned the signed contract and began 'interviewing' Howard Hughes and writing the autobiography.

In December 1971, the publishers announced the autobiography deal. Many people doubted the deal was real. Friends and work colleagues of Hughes claimed that Hughes would never reveal anything about his private life.

The evidence

Evidence showing that Irving was lying began to be gathered.

- Handwriting experts compared the 'Howard Hughes' signature on the contract to known copies of Hughes' signatures and to Irving's handwriting. They found that the signature on the contract had more similarities to Irving's handwriting than to Hughes's.

- A man claiming to be Howard Hughes contacted a journalist by phone saying that he knew nothing about the autobiography, had not agreed to its publication and had not been interviewed. Voice examination experts compared the voice to old recordings of Howard Hughes. Their findings were that the man on the phone was most likely Howard Hughes.

- The H. R. Hughes bank account in which the publisher's payments were deposited turned out to be owned by Hilda R. Hughes, not Howard R. Hughes. Hilda Hughes was later found to be Irving's wife, Edith.

- Most of the content of Irving's book was found to have been taken from an unpublished biography on Hughes.

Clifford Irving eventually confessed to the fraud once all the forensic evidence piled up against him. Irving received a two-and-a-half-year sentence and his wife received a two-year sentence. They were ordered to repay the US$750 000 to McGraw-Hill.

Clifford Irving carried out the Hughes hoax during the 1970s.

Investigating the investigators

Most forensic investigators are police members who have a science, engineering or other relevant university degree. Outside experts are also involved. The following experts are just some of the experts involved in forensic investigations and technologies.

Audio-visual experts

Audio-visual experts are physicists or computer engineers who examine images, sound recordings and multimedia.

Scene-of-crime officers

Scene-of-crime officers (SOCOs) are specially trained police and other professionals who search the crime scene for evidence.

Document examiners

Document examiners are people trained in analysing all aspects of a document, including writing samples, paper, ink and printer type.

Expert witnesses

Expert witnesses are senior police officers, forensic investigators and other professionals who present evidence in court. They present evidence in a way that the judge and jury can clearly understand.

Forensic photographers

Forensic photographers are police who photograph or video the crime scene and evidence to visually preserve it.

Forensic pathologists

Forensic pathologists are medical doctors who specialise in carrying out autopsies. Their main role is to determine how, when and where a person died, but they also examine wounds on surviving victims. Pathologists often examine bloodstain patterns at the crime scene.

Glossary

admissible	accepted as evidence in court
ballistics	scientific study of firearms, bullets, cartridge cases and projectiles
beneficiary	person who benefits from something
contamination	being made impure by something being added
databases	computer systems that hold data, such as fingerprints, that can be accessed by different people
impressions	marks, imprints or prints made by the pressure of an object on a surface
incident	violent, dangerous or criminal event
item of interest	object that may be a piece of evidence
pitch	high or low quality of a tone or sound
preserve	keep in the same condition
recluse	person who removes themselves from society and lives alone with very little outside contact
resolution	level of detail visible in an image
secure	make safe
tone	strength and vibrations of sound
trace evidence	evidence that is present in very small amounts only
unbiased	having no opinion for or against something

Index

A
alterations 18, 19, 21, 24
analysing evidence 12–13
audio specialists 24
audio-visual experts 12, 30

B
ballistics unit 12
Bell Telegraph Laboratories 25
blackmail 16

C
chain of custody 11, 14
chemicals 17, 18, 19
cheques 16, 18, 19
collecting evidence 8–11
crash investigation team 13

D
databases 26
date tags 18
defence team 15
deletions 19
detectives 6, 7
document examination 12, 16, 19, 22
document examiners 21, 22, 23, 30
dyes 17, 18, 23

E
electronic crime 23
electronic documents 23
evidence 4, 5, 6, 7, 8–11, 12–13, 14–15, 25, 26, 29, 30
evidence analysis 12–13
evidence collection 8–11
expert witnesses 14, 15, 30

F
facial recognition software 26
fakes 16
fax machines 22
Federal Bureau of Investigation (FBI) 25
fibres 17
fingerprints 8, 12, 26
forensic investigators 8, 12, 14, 26, 30
forensic photographers 30
forensic science centres 11, 12, 13
forgeries 16, 17, 19, 21, 23

G
glues 17
grid search 9

H
handwriting analysis 12, 20–21, 29
Hughes, Howard 28, 29

I
image enhancement 27
imperfections 22
impressions 8, 23
imprints 23
inks 12, 16, 18, 19, 30
Irving, Clifford 28, 29

L
line search 9

M
money 16, 17

P
paper 12, 16, 17, 19, 22, 23, 30
photocopiers 18, 22
photographs 7, 8, 10, 14, 26
piracy 23
pixels 27
print analysis 22
printers 18, 22, 30
prosecution team 15

R
resolution 27

S
scene-of-crime officers (SOCOs) 7, 30
searching the crime scene 9
securing the crime scene 6
sound waves 24
spectrograph 25
spiral search 9

T
television shows 5, 12, 16, 24, 27
trace evidence unit 12
typewriters 18, 22

V
video security footage 26, 27
voice analysis 24, 25, 29
voiceprints 25

W
watermarks 17
wills 16, 18, 19

Z
zone search 9